A Different Species of Breathing
The Poetry of Sue Goyette

A Different Species of Breathing
The Poetry of Sue Goyette

Selected
with an
introduction by
Bart Vautour
and an
interview with Sue Goyette
by Erin Wunker

LAURIER POETRY SERIES

WILFRID LAURIER
UNIVERSITY PRESS

Wilfrid Laurier University Press acknowledges the support of the Canada Council for the Arts for our publishing program. We acknowledge the financial support of the Government of Canada through the Canada Book Fund for our publishing activities. Funding provided by the Government of Ontario and the Ontario Arts Council. This work was supported by the Research Support Fund.

Library and Archives Canada Cataloguing in Publication

Title: A different species of breathing : the poetry of Sue Goyette / selected with an introduction by Bart Vautour and an interview with Sue Goyette by Erin Wunker.
Other titles: Poems. Selections (2023)
Names: Goyette, Sue, author. | Vautour, Bart, editor. | Wunker, Erin, interviewer.
Series: Laurier poetry series.
Description: Series statement: Laurier poetry series | Includes bibliographical references.
Identifiers: Canadiana (print) 2022049827X | Canadiana (ebook) 20220498318 |
    ISBN 9781771125819 (softcover) | ISBN 9781771125826 (EPUB) |
    ISBN 9781771125833 (PDF)
Classification: LCC PS8563.O934 A6 2023 | DDC C811/.54—dc23

Front cover image: *Variable Retention* by Lou Sheppard. This is a graphic score of composed spectrograms (sound images) of vulnerable, threatened, and endangered bird species found in a proposed clear cut (variable retention) in southwestern Nova Scotia / Kespukwitk, Mi'kma'ki. These bird species include Bicknell's Thrush, Canada Warbler, Common Nighthawk, Eastern Wood-Pewee, Eastern Whip-poor-will, Olive-sided Flycatcher, and Rusty Blackbird.
Cover design by Gary Blakeley.
Interior design by Mike Bechthold.

© 2023 Wilfrid Laurier University Press
Waterloo, Ontario, Canada
www.wlupress.wlu.ca

This book is printed on FSC® certified paper, contains post-consumer fiber and other controlled sources, is manufactured using renewable energy-biogas and processed chlorine free.

Printed in Canada

Wilfrid Laurier University Press is located on the Haldimand Tract, part of the traditional territories of the Haudenosaunee, Anishnaabe, and Neutral Peoples. This land is part of the Dish with One Spoon Treaty between the Haudenosaunee and Anishnaabe Peoples and symbolizes the agreement to share, to protect our resources, and not to engage in conflict. We are grateful to the Indigenous Peoples who continue to care for and remain interconnected with this land. Through the work we publish in partnership with our authors, we seek to honour our local and larger community relationships, and to engage with the diversity of collective knowledge integral to responsible scholarly and cultural exchange.

Table of Contents

Foreword

I am happy to serve as the general editor for the Laurier Poetry Series, the development and growth of which I have followed from its early days. My gratitude goes to Neil Besner and Brian Henderson, who conceived of the Laurier Poetry Series in 2002 as a way to offer a more robust selection of a single poet's work than could be found in an anthology. In 2004, the Laurier Poetry Series launched the first volume, Catherine Hunter's selection of the poems of Lorna Crozier, *Before the First Word*. Neil served as General Editor for all volumes until he was joined in 2016 by Brian, when he left his role as WLU Press's Director. In an act of commitment to poetry publication that is nothing short of inspiring, the Laurier Poetry Series expanded to a list of thirty-three fascinating titles under their leadership.

The retirement of the original editors has given me a surprising historical jolt. But thinking historically is a good way to revisit the original plans for the series, and to think towards the future. Under my editorial eye, the series will retain its original aim to produce volumes of poetry made widely available to new readers, including undergraduate students at universities or colleges, and to a general readership who wish for "more poetry in their poetry." WLU Press also retains its commitment to produce beautiful volumes and to alert readers to poems that remain vital to thinking about urgencies of the contemporary moment. It is a reality that poetry books are produced in smaller print runs and often on a shoestring, and as a consequence, original collections of poetry tend to go out of print too quickly and far too precipitously. The series has the added goal of bringing poems from out-of-print collections back into the public eye and the public discourse. The Press's commitment to the work of literary studies includes choosing editors for each volume who can reflect deeply on the body of work, as well as inviting original afterwords from the poets themselves.

As we embark on this next turn of the series, access is our watchword. Canadian literature has undeniably had a checkered history of exclusionary practices, so who gets the nod and who takes part in discussions—as readers and as writers—of Canadian poetry? In the classroom, it is my privilege and my task to introduce a generation of students to the practice of reading poetry as a vital thread in cultural, social, and political conversations, conversations that challenge ideas · about Canada and seek to illuminate and bring to consciousness better futures. For that work, I want access to as many voices on the page, and as robust a selection of poems from those voices, as I can get my hands on. This is the language of the bibliophile, the craver of books, the person whose pedagogical pleasure comes from putting poetry books into the hands of others and saying, simply, "Read this, and we'll talk." Multi-author anthologies do not always usefully demonstrate to readers how a poet's work shifts and changes over the years, nor do they always display the ways that a single poet's poems speak to and with and sometimes usefully against one another. I want at my elbow, in every discussion, inside and outside the classroom, our best poetic practitioners. I want books that offer not just a few poems, but dozens: selected volumes not only by the splashiest prize winners but also significantly by poets who have been carrying a full cultural backpack for decades. I also want to showcase new and prolific voices who have taken off like rockets. For this, I am grateful for the chance to bring these poets to you, or bring them back to you. Turn is sometimes a return and sometimes a revolution. Neil and Brian started this series off with a bang, and now it's time to light another fuse.

The volume you hold in your hands sizzles. Read this, and we'll talk.

—*Tanis MacDonald*
General Editor

Biographical Note

Sue Goyette was born in Sherbrooke, Quebec, but is now a long-time Nova Scotian. She published her first collection of poetry, *The True Names of Birds*, in 1998 with Brick Books. She also published her second and third collections—*Undone* (2004) and *Outskirts* (2011)—with Brick Books. The publication of her fourth collection, *Ocean*, in 2013 represented a shift in publishers to Gaspereau Press, based in Nova Scotia. Gaspereau Press published *The Brief Reincarnation of a Girl* in 2015, *Penelope: In First Person* in 2017, *Anthesis: A Memoir* in the spring of 2020, and *Solstice 2020: An Archive* in the spring of 2021. Recently, Sue was named Halifax's Municipal Poet Laureate (2020–23).

Her poetry has won the Pat Lowther Memorial Award, the Atlantic Poetry Prize, the CBC Literary Prize for Poetry, the Earle Birney Prize, the ReLit Award, the Nova Scotia Established Artist Recognition Award, the National Magazine Award (Silver), the Atlantic Independent Booksellers Choice Award, and the Bliss Carman Poetry Award. *The True Names of Birds* (now in its seventh printing) was shortlisted for the Governor General's Literary Award for poetry, and *Ocean* (also in its seventh printing) was shortlisted for the 2014 Griffin Poetry Prize, perhaps Canada's most prestigious prize for poetry. *Ocean* was the recipient of the 2015 Lieutenant Governor of Nova Scotia Masterworks Arts Award. Sue was guest editor of the 2013 edition of *The Best Canadian Poetry in English*. She was a judge for the 2017 Griffin Poetry Prize and edited *The Griffin Anthology* (House of Anansi Press, 2017). *Ocean* was recently translated by Georgette Leblanc, an Acadian Nova Scotian and Canada's Parliamentary Poet Laureate (2018–19). The French-language translation, *Océan*, was published by Les Éditions Perce-Neige in 2019. *Ocean* has also been translated into Spanish and German.

In addition to her collections of poetry, she has also published a novel, *Lures* (HarperCollins, 2002). Met with critical acclaim, *Lures* was shortlisted for the 2003 Thomas Head Raddall Atlantic Fiction Award, which is awarded each year for a novel or a book of short fiction written by a full-time resident of Atlantic Canada. Sue has recently edited, and provided an introduction for, *Resistance*, an anthology of poetry about sexual assault and abuse published by University of Regina Press.

Sue has been a mentor to many, both formally and informally. Formally speaking, she has had a significant role in the Writers' Federation of Nova Scotia Alistair MacLeod Mentorship Program, working with emerging authors to hone their craft. She has also participated in the MFA Creative Writing Program at University of Guelph and has offered master classes at Concordia University. Informally, she has counselled many, many of Nova Scotia's writers on building a writerly life.

Sue has also served as the Writer-in-Residence at Dalhousie University and the University of Prince Edward Island. She has been teaching students in the Creative Writing Program at Dalhousie University since 2007. She has also been faculty at the Banff Centre for the Arts, the Sage Hill Writing Experience, the Blue Heron Writing Workshop at St. Francis Xavier University, Mount Saint Vincent University, and the NSCAD School of Extended Studies, and has worked for the Writers' Federation of Nova Scotia. Sue completed a graduate degree in Women and Gender Studies at Saint Mary's University in 2021.

Introduction

Sue Goyette and the Building of Intimate Publics

> There are more ways to abandon a child
> than to leave them at the mouth of the woods.
>
> —Sue Goyette, "The True Names of Birds"

From the very beginning of Sue Goyette's published work—starting with the opening poem of her debut collection and its proposition of a multitude of ways to abandon a child—the poet reaches behind a reader's sternum and pulls. Goyette gets our attention that way. And that attention endures: it forces a reckoning with the large and small labours of witnessing the world and our locations within it. Goyette's vision is that of a feminist witness who understands the ongoing persistence of lives needing attention and the warranty of another's care. Whether the lives are those of children, partners, parents, plants, mythic figures, whole ecosystems, or a more general and ever-changing public, they deserve the attention that an engaged poetry can give. And Goyette gives them—and by extension us—the intimate attention of poetic care. Across the many and multiple subjects of Goyette's poetry, we see witnessing and care remain fundamental.

Goyette's first collection of poetry, *The True Names of Birds* (1998), announces itself as a collection that is intimately concerned with the life of "the poet." The collection doesn't simply recast the figure of the poet with a different actor, but instead raises "the poet" up in a manner that adds to larger feminist renovations of who gets to take up the mantle and capacity of "the poet." *The True Name of Birds* asks how we culturally attend to that figure and it reconceptualizes the lyric mode poetry might employ. It also demands the subjects of a poem be torn away from individualized expectation that has typically been coded as masculine. In *The True Name of Birds* the poet that Goyette presents is one who brings her life into the life of poetry. While this poet certainly makes room for wonder and reflection (if not always repose), the stuff of life can always be found close to the centre of the poem too: bikes, old shoes, broken crayons, cups of tea left half-full, and "the special stick for rescuing worms drying on the pavement." In "For the Unrejoiced" Goyette terms these quotidian objects as "need-more-milk-and-bread words." This collection also names children, specifically, as fitting chaperones for poetry: "Ryan" and "Robyn" enter into the poetry not as everyday words describing the things that surround a life, but as constituent of poetry and the wonder of language itself. Children become both poetic and the poetry itself. These are Goyette's children, sure, and in *The True Names of Birds* they are also the children of poetry and language itself. We see, in "Again to Be a Daughter," the desire for the poet to not only take up the subject position of the child, but specifically the "daughter" who would "only know now"— at the *end* of a poem much concerned with motherhood—that bringing the mother "something cool to drink" is as profound a poetic imperative as any other. While the inventiveness and wonder of children mark a sort of poetic longing (if not envy) throughout the collection, children are also marked as working in multiple ways, as not only the ideal inventors of a "truer" poetic nomenclature, but also the active listeners who are attentive to the best poetics of their caregivers. In "Solstice and the Other Long Days" we get a glimpse of the work children can do for poetry and poetry for children, as readers are asked to contemplate "how close / to the edge of all those steep places our children went, / just to hear echoes of our reassurance." While this reciprocal poetic relation between children and caregiver acts as a foundation for what has become a clear trajectory that traces multiple modes of care throughout Goyette's career, we can begin to see that relationship of care expand already in this first book. In "Women Drinking Tea or Tequila" a collective emerges wherein the poet declares: "We are each other's witnesses." Here Goyette writes of women finding ways to narrate subjectivity while also giving care to others for that same task. Further, it is this witnessing, care, and witnessing of care that becomes the throughline and the poetics: "Together / our names spell this poem, we are all in here, emerald green, ice blue." *The True Names of Birds* begins Goyette's publication history, and it also marks the accumulation of a readership and recognition. The collection was shortlisted for the 1999 Gerald Lampert, Pat Lowther, and Governor General's awards. *The True Name of Birds* marked the arrival of an important poet and has been reprinted many times. As Patrick Lane suggests, "This is a collection to begin everything with, a cure for silence, secrets that arrive with a steady eloquence" (n.p.).

With her 2004 collection, *Undone*, Goyette expands her poetics both figuratively and physically. While maintaining a focus on witnessing and care, her public takes up more space in the lives of those around her— while still encompassing the most intimate. Coincident with this figural expansion, Goyette makes more use of an elongated line, prompting a material change in the book's format to a landscape binding. As an example of this expanding public, in "For Women Who Cry When They Drive," the lives of those witnessed in the intimate act of crying are not the lives of those set around an intimate kitchen table as in "Women Drinking Tea or Tequila," but in the public spaces of highways and against the auditory backdrop of public broadcasting. Here, we see a continued expansion of poetry's scope to include what we might call intimate publics. Within these intimate publics, Goyette continues to build recognition of and admiration for the solidity of language doing its humble and extraordinary labour when we allow ourselves to get out of the way and let it actually accomplish that work. In "Back When We'd Try Anything to Fix It" Goyette warns of overdetermining language: she gives us the case wherein a mention of "seagulls" and "distance" was marked as an indecipherable metaphor or symbolic divining:

[...] I remember trying to figure out

what you meant, what was being foreshadowed
and would follow. Anything spoken with the word
distance in it used to interest me greatly. I thought something
sacred was being said, some celestial message

for me and the direction my life should take. Now I think
you were talking about seagulls, the way their bodies
disappear in snow only to reappear against sky and finally, now,
that's enough. Beauty isn't as hard to reach as I used to think.

Demystifying the communicative act, while also insisting on its core poetic function of astonishment, Goyette comes to the point where beauty "isn't as hard to reach" when you let language thrive in the work of thick, precise, and fresh description alongside an active mode of listening to others. Goyette also extends her intimate publics to a wide-ranging *poetic* public wherein she variously responds to the work of other poets across time and space. *Undone* contains poems that respond to the work of poets such as e.e. cummings, Jack Gilbert, Miguel Hernández, Pablo Neruda, Edna St. Vincent Millay, Dylan Thomas, and John Thompson. With "On Hearing Elizabeth Bishop Read Her 'Crusoe in England'" Goyette makes familiar the voice of Elizabeth Bishop and, in so doing, exemplifies in the work of "the poet" a commitment to becoming interwoven with the poetry of others, thus expanding and providing care for the work of poetry. With such forceful attention paid to a vast and varied chorus of poets, Goyette demands her readers pay attention to more than the poem before them: she asks us to pay close attention to a wider congregation of poetics.

Goyette's final collection published with Brick Books, *Outskirts* (2011), gathers more people into her intimate public. In "Heavy Metal Night at Gus's Pub," the children who are poetry's best people in her first collections become the precious and vulnerable-making subjects the poet places in relation to the people of her public encounter: "I want to tell all the long bearded boys that I have a boy just like them" and that "I want to tell the girls wearing black leather chaps with matching bras, poised to shove, / to check and boulder, that I have a girl and though she closes her eyes when she twirls, / I've seen her avalanche." What is remarkable here is the poet's desire to be seen by others in relation to her most precious connections—a boy and a girl both like and unlike the patrons of an intimate and vital Halifax music venue. We find an increasingly extended public emerge in these poems, including "The New Mothers," with its anxious collective of new parents rendezvousing "to master *Goodnight Moon*," and "Mission," wherein a small band of strangers come together to build a (mischievous) community with a task: "It will be up to us," her group tells in collective voice: "We'll have to knock on neighbours' doors, we'll have to wake them. / No, really. We will have to wake them up. Then we'll have to run." Goyette constructs community in poetry as a set of relations among people. But she doesn't just bring humans into close relation in poetry; this collection marks an increasingly articulated and relational eco-poetics too. Though examples of ecological concern certainly show up in earlier collections, it is with *Outskirts* that we get whole sequences of poems engaging with the ecological. As the ecological poetic engagement ramps up in her work, it is important to make clear that Goyette's eco-poetics doesn't resemble the remains of a well-worn Romanticism that sets the so-called "natural" apart from the human public she so clearly foregrounds. There aren't any light and airy musings on distant views here. Rather, her eco-poetic attention in *Outskirts* is an extension of her intimate publics and, most notably, of the cityscape of Halifax as well as the place of public policy in environmental management (as in "Clear-Cut"). With this collection, Goyette sets the stage for what will become a long, detailed, and breathtaking biography of the water at the city's edge in her 2013 collection, *Ocean*.

Ocean marks a shift to Goyette publishing with Gaspereau Press, a small press with a focus on Atlantic Canadian literature and a long history in the art of making beautiful books. With the change to Gaspereau, we see in Goyette's career a move away from collections of individual (though interconnected) poems to publishing books in a poetic mode that could be classified as unified conceptual projects or even book-length long poems. In *Ocean*, Goyette manages to write a history—or a biography—of an ocean who has made active choices and shaped human lives. *Ocean* is not just a history of human use of the ocean; it is a poetic account of the ocean as a cultural formation with subjectivity that is sometimes oppositional, sometimes benevolent. Written as a long poem intimately committed to a formal engagement with the couplet stanza (with enough deviation to suggest she wants us to notice and think through the couplet form), *Ocean*'s project is one that asks readers to reorient themselves in relation to what they *think* they know of the ocean's role in social, cultural, and political development. As Pamela Banting suggests, "this poem is a way of exploring the idea of belonging—to the shore, to the ocean, to seawater, to the planet, to one another, and to a community" (123). With a collective address that speaks for a constantly shifting we, the book tells of an active ocean working on us:

We laughed at first. At the thought. Like it was
a joke. Imagine, the ocean basting us. But how often

had we walked into its salted air then licked our arms
to taste it later? We were being seasoned. Lightly.

Indeed, *Ocean* met a wide readership upon publication and continues to gather readers. *Ocean* was winner of the 2015 Lieutenant Governor of Nova Scotia Masterwork Arts Award and finalist for the 2014 Griffin Poetry Prize. The collection received a French-language translation in 2019 and was published by Éditions Perce-Neige. It was translated by Georgette LeBlanc, a former Canadian Parliamentary Poet Laureate (2018–19), and received the Governor General's Award, Translation Category, in 2020.

Goyette's publications after *Ocean*—*The Brief Reincarnation of a Girl* (2015), *Penelope: In First Person* (2017), *Anthesis: A Memoir* (2020), and *Solstice 2020: An Archive* (2021)—track an ongoing attentiveness to affect and care in an ever-expanding creation and support of intimate publics. While certainly evident in earlier works, these more recent collections amplify Goyette's focus on connection and making intimate social relations outside of expected realms. These books also mark what might be best described as the poet's intensifying attention to trauma and reciprocity and the ways in which poetry can engage with these experiences on individual and collective levels. While writing these works, Goyette also completed a Master of Arts in Women and Gender Studies. Goyette's graduate work is on trauma-informed pedagogy and considers methods of interspecies connection. In the "Introduction" to her Master's thesis Goyette cites the importance of radical feminist trauma theorists such as Bonnie Burstow, Laura S. Brown, Ann Cvetkovich, Rosemary Barnes, and Susan Schellenberg to her own thinking.

Goyette's poetic figurations within *The Brief Reincarnation of a Girl* hinge on and take cues from the death of a real girl, Rebecca Riley, who at the age of four was found dead from an overdose of pharmaceuticals prescribed to her for ADHD and bipolar disorder. Riley's parents were charged and convicted of murder, while her prescribing psychiatrist continued in medical practice. The case, which made national headlines in the United States, was framed by media as one in which Big Pharma and parental neglect were to blame. Goyette's poetry asks a wider and different set of questions, shifting and widening the gaze from the egregious failures of medical and social systems to the girl herself. The collection, which is written in dense stanzaic lineation, personifies everything, asking what might happen if we observed and listened with compassion and curiosity. In *Poetic Investigations* Paul Naylor develops his notion of the "investigative lyric" which queries absences in history in order to shift or elevate the subject of lyric voice. The aim of the investigative lyric is both recuperative and sleuth-like. It is looking for what and who was left out.

The opening lines of Goyette's work demonstrate the investigative lyric in action:

> The girl refused to be afraid when she climbed
> on high things. Her mother shaved the legs of the furniture
> and, along with some cough syrup, stewed it
> with a few of the girl's father's beer caps. The girl spit
> a whole parade's worth of bicycle bells back at her
> and pranced around in her diaper.

Goyette centres the girl both in and out of time. Her fearlessness and joy are met with surreal and sinister responses suited to a twenty-first century adaptation of a Grimm tale. Each time the girl's exuberance is framed as excessive an adult in the tale is positioned as malevolent, out of touch, or deeply unfit. The mother "sat in the closet, lit a candle, and located the doctor with binoculars." The doctor suggests "more conventional medication, the girl sounded bipolar / and should be on a leash." The more outrageous the adult intervention, the more resilient the girl. The result, throughout the course of the collection, is to elevate the small child up out of the torture of her life and into a place where a reader can encounter who she might have been, had she been well-held. Goyette renders this elevation through consistent allegorical personification of animals and objects. Poverty is a witness in the courtroom. Prescription pads have agendas. And a stuffed bear can move beyond the confines of its polyester body to find its wildness, and in so doing meet the girl in her loneliness and neglect and teach her to fish for her own precious heart.

If *The Brief Reincarnation of a Girl* introduces the investigative lyric into Goyette's poetic oeuvre, then *Penelope: In First Person* anchors it as a central tool. *Penelope* is a rewriting of *The Odyssey*. In the original epic Penelope, Odysseus's wife, is allotted scant mention. Her role is to stay at home, wait for Odysseus, weave, and hold off the tsunami of suitors who come to claim her affection. Not so in Goyette's work. Here, Penelope is the central lyric speaker. The poems of *Penelope: In First Person*, which are organized by couplet stanzas, depend on Penelope to move the narrative forward with epic attention, care, and vigilance that counterbalances the masculine epic of the original. Unlike *The Brief Reincarnation of a Girl*, which moves time to make space for a lyric voice that is almost wholly erased and reimagines the potential of a life cut short, here time moves at the pace of domestic femininity:

I wake to visitors at the door. Can we get something
to drink? I'm asked. Dutifully, I call for more chairs.

Can we get something a little stronger? they say. They say,
can you make us a sandwich while you're up? Trees are felled

in the south lot for more chairs.

In this collection the demands on women and the expectations of
feminized domestic labour are the subjects of lyric investigation.
Penelope's duty, diligence, and skill are coupled with her exhaustion,
frustration, and grief. Again, personification serves to train the gaze and
attention of the reader. Take, for instance, a scene in which Penelope's son
Telemachus demands entrance to her chamber:

The door wakens to Telemachus. Let me in, it's told.
Its lock is diplomatic until attacked then will dutifully hold

to its bolts. Telemachus's shoulder tastes of boy
but his breath is loose with something amateurly hinged.

The mother is aided in her duties of care and forensic observation of a
child. The door helps create boundaries for Penelope against her adult
son's anger. It also witnesses Telemachus's childhood wounds and griefs
and offers a firm boundary against which to press them. The result of this
cavalcade of personification is palpable in its inherent proposition: what
if we added diligence and care to our set of tools we use to witness one
another? Published at the height of the #MeToo movement, *Penelope: In
First Person* appears, as Sina Queyras puts it, to be "exploring the idea of
voice—where does it come from?—and its relationship to syntax . . . It's a
kind of 'after lyric' or 'elevated lyricism'" (9). Indeed, near the end of the
collection the dutiful stanzaic couplets break:

I awake, I woke   am asked

reply and say:

(dutifullydutifullydutifullydutifullydutifully)

if anything
my loss is mortal and has been acting like a goddess.

While *Penelope* applies an investigative lyric to a canonical text of Western literature to make clear a feminist reimaging and remonstration, in her next collection, Goyette revisits and recasts both personal and literary expectations of framing trauma and earlier selves.

Anthesis: A Memoir continues Goyette's interest in connection, trauma, and reciprocity. The word "anthesis" indicates a blossoming. Within the blossoming is also *thesis*, or proposal. Bound together with memoir, the collection hypothesizes that blossoming is possible within the life story of the poet. In the preface that opens the collection, Goyette explains that the work was initiated as a part of her Master's thesis on trauma, memoir, and reciprocity. *Anthesis* introduces tactics of experimental poetics of erasure and procedure to engage with a semi-autobiographical novel, *Lures* (2002), which Goyette wrote and published nearly two decades prior. Goyette uses erasure techniques to return to and repurpose the work of the original novel, while procedure comes in the form of daily witnessing of the transplantation, blooming, and death of an agave plant in the Halifax Public Gardens. The result is poetry that moves between past and present to envision a future in which all creatures have the potential to bloom after experiences of individual and collective trauma. The tone for this iteration of collectivity and attention is set in the opening prose stanza:

Burning flowers: prepare for the next season. Low chimneys
dividing dispute between farther and pure fire; exhausted
silence startled into silence. The long lament south of the sinking: a
vivid and stubborn premonition. No one remembered the exodus
from family taking every day and all night. Smoldering for her
younger edge, always more and then towards. Is the girl leaving
an emergency? She was and barely looking away.

The implied collective, "burning flowers," are told how to steady themselves for change and renewal. A nuanced affective shift is ushered in, from "exhausted silence" to "silence" and a girl is re-met by her older self and accompanied from "an emergency" into her next season. By the end of the collection the girl, kept company by a collective of other "burning flowers," is able to meet a heretofore absent and wanting mother, and "each green" reaches for one another through, and despite, their traumas.

Written in the midst of global shared trauma, *Solstice 2020: An Archive* began as a daily poem written and published in a local Halifax daily newspaper—*The Coast*—leading up to the December solstice. Deep in the second wave of the Covid-19 pandemic, Goyette's poems function as modes of public witnessing and connection when no one could be together to metabolize shared fear and grief. The poems of this brief collection work in the occasional mode, marking days from the poet's perspective while reaching out to a local, national, and global community of readers. "December 6" addresses the anniversary of the murder of fourteen women on a university campus in 1989 by a misogynist by reminding readers "at the heart of mourning / is an inlet with small boats for us to row forward." Memory of communal grief may be the tool needed. "December 9," meanwhile, meditates on the origins of laughter while lamenting the distance between loved ones. If an archive is at its most basic a collection brought together to mark a stretch of time, then *Solstice* is an investigative archive that bears witness to a moment when, as darkness stretched into days and distance developed new definitions, poetry reminded readers of its power to connect.

Throughout her published career that has developed and sustained a poetics of witness and care, Sue Goyette has also extended that care to the larger project of fostering poetic community. But what is more, her poetics—her mode of watching, listening, safeguarding, wilding, and uplifting—builds more than just a poetic or readerly community. It creates and extends an intimate public beyond a wide readership to those who her readers might encounter in the everyday conditions of both joy and suffering: Goyette ask her readers to notice and care. For readers new to her work, the small selection that follows gives a glimpse into the myriad ways we can come together alongside the deep listening and steady insights of a tremendous poet.

—*Bart Vautour*

Works Cited

Banting, Pamela. "H₂Ocean: The Wet Ontology and Blue Ethics of Sue Goyette's *Ocean.*" *Studies in Canadian Literature / Études en littérature Canadienne* 45.2: 122–40.

Goyette, Sue. *Anthesis: A Memoir.* Gaspereau Press, 2020.

———. *The Brief Reincarnation of a Girl.* Gaspereau Press, 2015.

———. *Lures: A Novel.* HarperFlamingo Canada, 2002.

———. *Ocean.* Gaspereau Press, 2013.

———. *Océan* (French translation by Georgette Leblanc), Éditions Perce-Neige, 2019.

———. *Outskirts.* Brick Books, 2011.

———. *Penelope: In First Person.* Gaspereau Press, 2017.

———. *Solstice 2020: An Archive.* Gaspereau Press, 2021.

———. *The True Names of Birds.* Brick Books, 1998.

———. *Undone.* Brick Books, 2004.

Lane, Patrick. "This is a collection…" Back cover of *The True Names of Birds.* Brick Books, 1998.

Naylor, Paul. *Poetic Investigations: Singing the Holes in History.* Evanston: Northwestern UP, 1999.

Queyras, Sina. "Women, Epic, Live Wires: In Conversation with Sue Goyette." *Lemonhound 3.0* lemonhound.com, 12 Dec 2017. Web.

A Different Species of Breathing

from
The True Names of Birds
(1998)

The True Names of Birds

There are more ways to abandon a child
than to leave them at the mouth of the woods.
Sometimes by the time you find them, they've made up names
for all the birds and constellations, and they've broken
their reflections in the lake with sticks.

With my daughter came promises and vows
that unfolded through time like a roadmap and led me
to myself as a child, filled with wonder for my father
who could make sound from a wide blade of grass

and his breath. Here in the stillness of forest,
the sun columning before me temple-ancient,
that wonder is what I regret losing most; that wonder
and the true names of birds.

Again to Be a Daughter

Trees die from the top. With even just a hint of disease, they seed harder
then slowly start giving up leaves. And they don't die easy. My maple
takes up the whole livingroom window with its dying. It's exhausting

to watch the struggle when wind becomes tangled in its stillness. Sometimes
I have to pull the curtains over and turn on the lamp just to be able to read.
And there's nothing I can do. There are no recipes to stop death once it's started.

Beginnings seem easier, a pale pumpkin seed, earth. The dying maple's shadow
and my daughter pirouetting beneath it, throwing its seeds back up to the sky
to watch their lazy descent again. She won't notice how bare the top of the tree is

or hear it being pulled back to the ground. She sees only pumpkins. And believes
in fairy godmothers. If anything, motherhood has made me midnight; things
have turned back into what they were. I've outgrown my shoes. Trees turn

to seed. There must be something I can pass down to her. Some secret. I should
tell her to melt her broken crayons and turn them to candles to save for this darkness.
My mother had walked too far, her feet too tired to be able to run after me. She called

me in at dusk and waited for evening to call again. I only know now what she was
trying to show me; not just trees die from the top. I want to turn into a daughter
again. I'd know now to rub her feet and bring her something cool to drink.

Women Drinking Tea or Tequila

Here in the strange woods there are no paths, no trousered daddies
pointing out advice with the stems of their pipes. We've packed grocery
bags full of footprints for the trails we'll leave. Sat on suitcases

to close them and dipped our matches into wax. When we speak,
we walk in storyteller boots, timidly, trying not to crush the wild violets,
the strawberries. And slowly we become the heroines in our stories.

Flexing our strength for each other, then more wildly. Paint this,
one of us says, paint me moving finally from my childhood. She poses,
waving a gauzy scarf over her head. We see her every day, we know

she hangs her laundry out to dry the night before and is superstitious
about black cats and mirrors. We are each other's witnesses, each other's
crimes. Sitting around kitchen tables, circles of séance, we call

each other's dead. Half our lives spent chasing dragonflies that are furtive
and neon, always mating, always in flight; this half we spend helpless,
watching their colours fade as they die in our hands. We've learned

to be fish hooks, we've learned to be lakes. We bathe as though the room
is full of secret admirers, slowly, slowly, we wash out backs. I'm tired,
one of us says, sleep is just a welcome mat for travelling salesmen

with their bags of lost keys and their satchels of sick children. We slice
cucumbers for her eyes. Save our squeezed tea bags. Mornings are double-
jointed, wanting to go either way. Coaxing curtains open, we are steps

on a ladder to the window where daylight crouches, unsure. Together
our names spell this poem, we are all in here, emerald green, ice blue. Our lips
sewn shut. Damselfly, the devil's darning needle. No secrets ever get out.

from
Undone
(2004)

For Women Who Cry When They Drive

Blame it on CBC stereo if anyone asks. Blame it on
the viola. I did and it worked. I never even had to mention locksmiths

and lovers, how close the two are. I never had to name
each white-knuckle grip of his on the steering wheel. I'll name it here, though,

for you. Surrender and all its aliases. I feel at home in two places now.
One's here, the other in the library surrounded by reference books

to the stars. Driving doesn't help. But you already know that. Remember
when you stopped, pulled over on Cole Harbour Road and wept,

bowed to the wheel and the long road ahead, the long road behind. I tried
signalling, pulling over, but the traffic was stubborn. If you are reading this,

I did try to stop. The passing lanes of loss and love and the speed limit
to this life. I held you for days in my heart, dear sad woman in the dark green Volvo

next to the Dairy Queen, next to the Royal Bank, feeling like you have no choice.
And you don't. You don't, except to fasten your seat belt

and yield.

Back When We'd Try Anything to Fix It

One day, neither of us will be around to explain
the baby bathtub in the attic. It's the only thing up there.
Not even an attic, really, just a space
in the beams between roof and ceiling. We put it up there

on a day like this. Back then, everything was still intact. It was January
and snowing the way it does in Nova Scotia,
foreshadowed and followed by rain. I remember you
saying there is something about the way gulls look

against the snow that speaks of distance,
the blur of white bodies and the lift of their flight,
camouflage of the brief blizzard abandoned
for grey, indifferent sky. I remember trying to figure out

what you meant, what was being foreshadowed
and would follow. Anything spoken with the word
distance in it used to interest me greatly. I thought something
sacred was being said, some celestial message

for me and the direction my life should take. Now I think
you were talking about seagulls, the way their bodies
disappear in snow only to reappear against sky and finally, now,
that's enough. Beauty isn't as hard to reach as I used to think.

It was work, emptying the closet so you could get the ladder in.
We spoke about the clothes we don't wear any more. We spoke
about sweaters. Once in a while the wind would whirl up
and the window would whiten. We both agreed we were glad

to be inside. I remember holding the ladder, watching you disappear,
head first, through the attic opening. I remember thinking it was a type of birth
or rebirth, that something was changing or about to. But I used to
think that way. Life was often just verging on, about to, had to

get better. You kept talking after you disappeared into the attic,
as if the house had found its voice. *Are you sure*, it said, deeply,
forlornly. *Are you sure this will work?*

On Hearing Elizabeth Bishop Read Her "Crusoe in England"

Her voice is a blouse, crushed berries one
by one and then hours apart, open. Each word an island
with one kind of everything. O, I'm transported;

the archipelago of poem, her voice the bright blue
violet that creeps over everything, the ocean
of time around us, tide high and then retreating:

all the hemisphere's left-over loss at once. Was there
a moment when I actually chose this? Ten miles away,
a memory was being born and she swerved from its shore,

Mont d'Espoir, my despair, and navigated around the sinking
ship of family, the dreams of food and love. None of the books
have ever got it right. Her voice rained so much,

she built shelters of elegy around herself, invented umbrellas,
parasols. How, she wondered, could anyone want such things?
There were years, fifty-two miserable weeks in each, small volcanoes

she climbed thinking of caves, the faint glimmer of sky,
the way out. She'd been dyed early with bright red berries,
pale, pale Elizabeth, and then her mother didn't even know her.

When the birds leave her voice, all at once, the sound
is of a big tree in a strong wind. And other times, her voice
is a knife, begged, implored not to break. Every nick,

every scratch a cicatrice where once were leaves.
Her voice is a lantern, a spiked walking stick for climbing
over herself, it's a crucifix. It lives and, even now, delivers

the gossip, whispers the gospel, testimony of the long dead
according to the first chapter in the book of being stranded on a poem.

from
Outskirts
(2011)

Heavy Metal Night at Gus's Pub

I want to tell all the long bearded boys that I have a boy just like them. I have a boy and I imagine he too turns dance floors into a ricochet of minimum wage and dumpster diving, demolition derby in the size of a parking space shadowed by condos of parents and student loans, Superstore aprons and vibrating cellphones. I have a boy who dances. I want to tell the girls wearing black leather chaps with matching bras, poised to shove, to check and boulder, that I have a girl and though she closes her eyes when she twirls, I've seen her avalanche. The mosh pit is a boil of bodies and the singer is sliding down the banister of his voice, sending the screech of his descent directly into the mic as if it's a combination of girlfriend and government. I feel old. The floor is hard, the sneers sideways. When the singer falls back, his eyes closed, his hands holding the bird, the shark, the satellite at bay in his chest, all their hands reach up and carry him aloft like a gift or an offering. This is what I'm supposed to watch. I didn't know how it would happen, just that it would. My boy, my girl; a dance carried. And then gone.

The New Mothers

The new mothers are petting the giraffe neck of street lights,
cooing for more light. The streets are so unsafe.

And they're buckling up their tenderness. Oh the state
of the world! The new mothers have to attach umbrellas

to the things that move their children from here
to there. There is no more driving. The price of black ice

and yellow lights and gasoline. And the weather!
Fuck, the new mothers want to say. They have to wash their water

with water. The whole planet is at the window peering in
while the new mothers sit on the side of the bed.

They have to be wolves; they have to be golden-winged
warblers. Reminders, reminders.

They bury their phones for a minute of peace,
rendezvous to master *Goodnight Moon*

while the earth rings and rings beneath their feet.

Mission

We will meet at Gus's pub. In the darkest corner. We will gamble.

We will lose everything and then convince each other that losing is a winning experience.

We will be reminded to pay for our beers and will only have lighters. We've quit smoking but will not brag, will not say anything about poverty, that last weathered apple.

We will be asked to leave and will convince each other that leaving was our idea.

We will build a fire and sit around it. Halifax, we'll agree, is a hard-haunted town. The ghost of green, a long ago season.

We will not think silence is a takeover or we're in any way cheap labour. A winter without slush won't break our backs. It may be global warming but it isn't warm.

We will not say anything when a stranger says: *trees are fence enough.*

We will breathe that one in like a community.

We will put our hands on his forehead and conclude he's suffering from homesickness.

We will admit we're all suffering. *Oh home away from home. Oh trees. Oh planet.*

We will agree to do something. We'll compose a letter and then borrow a bike in this preposterous January, this winterless winter.

We will find our legs by riding the bike around the fire until the flames get greedy and snap like a shark.

We will want revenge and will burn our hands. The stranger will have to be carried. We will not complain of how heavy he is. He spoke of trees; he spoke of trees!

Our courage will flail then. The night so endangered. 9-1-1, 9-1-1!: it is the dead of winter and we can no longer see our breath. Rumours bruise our resolve. A car is alarming.

It will be up to us. We'll have to knock on neighbours' doors, we'll have to wake them. No really. We will have to wake them up. Then we'll have to run.

Clear-cut: one

Few wet depressions or aspects of a deciduous anxiety have roots

on the landscape as far-reaching as this new-growth fear. Over 95% of questions

harvested in Nova Scotia are answered using the technique of clear-cutting.

Clear-cutting a question involves cutting down virtually every standing curiosity

in a given neighbourhood, leaving an exposed heartland of vulnerable limbs

and tire ruts where a rich shady child once stood. Between 1975 and 1999,

almost 10,000 kilometers of Nova Scotian curiosity was slashed and burned,

which is more than a sixth of all the ideas in the province, and almost a quarter

of the exclamation marks and eurekas. (!!)

Bargaining

Here is the shadow of one small child. Here is the warmth from beneath
the sleeping cat. Here is the recorded breath from a rushed phone message

apologizing. Here is my daughter's bike. No, not my daughter.
Here is an oven mitt and a can opener. Here is the linden tree

hungover from drinking an entire collection of slow-moving seasons.
Here are the headlights of a car heading for the hospital.

Here is the baying of fear, and the coyote of awake. Here is a year
of routine. Here is saved gift wrap and string. Here is the teenage bellow

of boys, their hearts full moons demanding more sky. Here is the cloud
that resembles a small god lying with its back to us. Here is an hour
        of rain

and here is the thirst of anything captured. Here is my father's cough.
Here is a reading lamp and an address book of rivers. Here is an obituary

for a forest. Here is a briefcase full of diaries. Here is a suit to wear
to the trial. Here are small scissors to trim your hems. Here is a mirror.

Here is a photograph someone took of you when you weren't looking.
Here is memory pressed between pages, its petals translucent and dim.

Here are the promised jewels. Is that enough? We swim the channels
of your long hours so easily, and you, you hungry ocean,

when did you start being so tempted to keep us?

from
Ocean
(2013)

Prologue

We traded an accordion for hours of wood. We traded ladles
of sleep for some hammers and nails. We were setting out

to find the ocean. Our boats leaked. Our boats sank.
Our boats needed to be trained. We burned some of them

for light to build better boats. We turned some on their sides
and lived in them. Our children wrote their names in crooked

letters on the backs of them. Someone even cut a hole in the centre
of one and wore it suspended like pants. For awhile, everyone

wore boats. We built more fashionable boats. We wrote books
about building boats and then wrote more about the writing

of those books. Sure, we digressed but there was always plenty
of wood and a prime-time of hours to trade. A colony of us left

to watch how light moved over our boats. This demanded clocks.
We banged on our boats and howled and in this way created

the Calling of the Ocean ceremony. This became a holiday
with a feast and a fire. Dancing. Our population almost doubled

when we drank the fermented fruit and holidayed. We cleared more
land to store the boats. The boatbuilding industry was booming.

We eventually even cooked our boats and ate their ash
then dreamt at night of fish. Fish. Those strange contraptions

that don't need air. Little wallets swimming just out of reach.

We soon had an orchestra of boats and the songs
that sailed through us put the stars in the sky.

Of course, we were nowhere near the ocean. Our trees
were nuns at the edge of our plans, praying for us

in their way. And our rocks were mysteries we tried solving
but in these parts, the rocks are as stubborn as sisters and held

their tongues. We corded off part of a field beyond our beds
where the right combination of drink and wind

would leave us feeling oceanated. This land later became
a church then later, a music hall. Sacred. There were expeditions

to find the ocean. The reports given upon return always involved
leaping animals and thirst. There was first a swamp of skyscrapers

to cross, a swarm of bankers. There were small shields
called briefcases and banks where you had to wait to be given

what belonged to you in the first place. At this point,
the bigger boats became stages and these journeys would be acted out

for everyone to see. Often children would be cast as bankers
shielding themselves with those briefcases. They'd run around at a silent

movie speed, begging everyone for more money. I played a skyscraper
but my arms got tired so I was replaced. Once I played a tree.

You're not praying hard enough, the audience heckled.

Two

It won every staring contest. Would laugh
at our jokes. It was the original god of hypnosis

and made us all feel sleepy. Over time, it became
a breed of static, an out-of-service channel broadcasting

beyond our buildings. If we drove to its feet,
it wasn't to confront it, but more to adjust

our own reflections, straighten out our hearts with the old
if-you-know-what's-good-for-you talk. Sure, our grandmothers

insisted on throwing in gifts of false teeth and single shoes
but reverence was considered a form of weakness

and we decided the ocean was a daring but
equally fashionable accessory for our vacation wardrobe.

The art of complaint was perfected when we first took note
of its temperature.

Seven

We had laughed at first. At the thought. Like it was
a joke. Imagine, the ocean *basting* us. But how often

had we walked into its salted air then licked our arms
to taste it later? We were being seasoned. Lightly. Of course we rebelled,

refusing to be in its roasting pan. But we had never encountered anything
so stubborn. It was worse than a mountain, its altitude

ranging in the upper echelon of *I know you are but what am I?*
And it was stoic, like a four-year-old la, la, la-ing. I can't hear you, it said.

The artists claimed it was the quintessential canvas.
Call it love, they insisted, and look how love persists. The widows said:

call it death or call it loneliness. Whatever it was, it was vast and swam
in its lane at the edge of our town without ever resting. It shouldn't have

come as such a surprise then, at how tender we were all becoming
and how close we were cooked to tears.

Fifty-Six

Filmmakers had started making films of the ocean
in 3D. Scratch and sniff coastal cards were sold

at lottery booths. Material for dresses was cut with the froth
of tide in mind. We had wanted the ocean to be the new

flavour, the new sound. We'd drive for miles to get a glimpse
of it because, let's face it, it revitalized the part of us

we kept rooting for, that apple seed of energy that defied
multiple choice career options. The ocean had egged the best part

of us on. And it scared us. We never knew what it was thinking
and spent thousands on specialists who could make predictions.

And the predictions always required hard hats and building permits,
furrowed eyebrows and downward trends. Why is it so hard

to trust something that leaps, disappears and then reappears
spouting more light? When had our hearts become badly behaved

dogs we had to keep the screen door closed to? Have you ever run
along its shore, the pant of it coming closer? And that feeling

that yipped inside of you, the Ginger Rogers of your feet, your ability
to not get caught then, yes, get soaked. Didn't you feel like it was

part of your pack? When it whistled, whatever it is in you
that defies being named, didn't that part of you perk up?

And didn't you let it tousle you to the ground,
let it clean between your ears before it left you?

Wasn't that all right? That it left you? That we all will?

from
The Brief Reincarnation
of a Girl
(2015)

One

The girl refused to be afraid when she climbed
on high things. Her mother shaved the legs of the furniture
and, along with some cough syrup, stewed it
with a few of the girl's father's beer caps. The girl spit
a whole parade's worth of bicycle bells back at her
and pranced around in her diaper. The mother sat in the closet,
lit a candle, and located the doctor with binoculars.
The doctor, appearing as a bathrobe, urged
the mother to slap the girl with her slippers then take her
pulse. The girl had begun to growl which was upsetting
the cats. The mother upped the dosage of bottle caps
and added some baby Aspirin. The doctor suggested
more conventional medication, the girl sounded bipolar
and should be on a leash. What they didn't know
was that the girl had collected enough stickers
to reward the universe. She had a blanket and a bear.
She had resolved that when she got up from the floor
that last time, she'd be in another time zone
with better tasting furniture and a door that closed.

Fifteen

The girl's ghost was not necessarily a ghost
but more a representative of the girl's curiosity.
She moved with an ease that belied her death
and sat between her parents. The fire on her father's
crotch immediately went out and her mother's hold
on her water glass lightened. The girl wanted her bear.
She wanted to hold the bear to her heart and hear
for herself. Why would she believe anything
they told her? She could trust the bear. The times it insisted
she was in a forest and would soon come to its edge.
She didn't understand why her mouth was filled
with sand and kept emptying it like a shoe.
She couldn't taste the window she put her tongue to
so tried licking it like a popsicle. It wasn't that she missed
her mother and father, she just liked the cooking smell
of their clothes and thought she was hungry. Her daycare
teacher kept trying to hand her flowers but when she
reached out to take them, her teacher busied herself
with the Kleenex they'd turn into and wouldn't look up.

Forty

The girl's bear heard the ghost of the girl's roar. The bear
had been sleeping. Normally, the sunlight would guide
the bear from her cave and she would then amble through
the woods until she came to the crumbling edge where the girl
lived, but there was no light to guide the bear now.
She pawed at the dark but couldn't find an opening and so bellowed
back to the ghost of the girl a message that the bear
would soon be there. The ghost of the girl standing on the chair
snarled back to the bear that the father had his rifle out
and the bear was safer in its cave. The bear missed the girl's heart,
the bear told the ghost of the girl, but so did the ghost of the girl.
What was it like? the ghost of the girl asked, and the bear
said it was like silver fish in a river, each beat sure and strong
and swimming with the current. How did the bear find the girl?
the ghost of the girl wanted to know. By smell, by the honey smell
of the girl the bear had found the girl lying there that last time,
on the floor without her heart.

Fifty-Eight

The bear had the ghost of the girl
in her arms when the judge came out
of his quarters. They looked at each other.
The idea of justice hung between them
like flypaper. They ignored poverty
and the smacking sounds it was making, feasting
off the trap. The bear put her head close to the ghost
of the girl's mouth and listened. She tasted
what the ghost said and then risked the sting
of many bees to put her snout in the hive
of the courtroom. I claim this girl, she said.
The judge nodded. She's always been mine,
the bear said and, again, the judge nodded, bowing
slightly. She was given to me. The bear tasted the silence
that met these words. Its broth was clear but without the fortitude
of meat. Poverty snuck up behind the bear and tried raking
her shadow with its fork. Without exertion, the bear
made ribbon of its pelt, tossing it to the father who laughed.
Again. This laugh was a kissing cousin to the laugh
of the morning the girl had been found. It was as inappropriate
as a party hat. The bear pulled her lips back and showed
her teeth. Her growl was as low and effective as forced air heating.
The judge used paperwork to deal with the drafts.

Fifty-Nine

When the mother and bear faced each other, the bear snouted
at the word *mother* like a carcass, spent and boned. The mother
tried protecting her wishbone with her high school yearbook.
She inhaled deeply and held in her fear until she was stoned enough
to see headlights. Someone was tapping on her eardrum
with a rack of antlers. She couldn't hear words for the voices.
The bear had pulled the last velour off the word *mother*
and the memory of the girl was fading and then broken.
Carla felt something shift. She couldn't name what she had lost
but it had been lambswool soft and now her bones were grinding together
before fusing stiff. Someone was speaking then lifting her arm
to guide her. She stood and allowed herself to be led.
She had lost her tongue, she wanted to tell them. Briefly, she was
outside, the sky an endless grocery list of clouds. A maple tree shimmered
more laughter as her head was being lowered, as she was being put
into the back of a van. Her mother was waiting for her
with photos of Carla as a girl. You see, I never understood
what you had found so funny. Delighting in every damn thing,
her mother told her. Her father cuffed her to a metal pole
and injected her with his pipe smoke. None of your sass,
he said. Carla leaned back and heard a girl say something to her
so she bent closer to hear. The girl was lying
on a blanket, dishevelled and thin. Isn't she pretty, momma,
she said holding up a bear. Momma? Carla tried saying, grieving
her tongue, who is this momma?

from
Penelope: In First Person
(2017)

I wake to visitors at the door. Can we get something
to drink? I'm asked. Dutifully, I call for more chairs.

Can we get something a little stronger? they say. They say,
can you make us a sandwich while you're up? Trees are felled

in the south lot for more chairs. The care dutifully given
to joints and spindles sacrificed, the carpenters forced

to assemble rudimentary stools then boxes. Constrained by
protocol, I count the visitors slightly but they are that jammed in,

I lose track of their legs. By week's end, the demand to be seated
so unruly, the carpenters are delivering stumps, then entire logs.

I wake to a swarm of suitors
and though everyone insists they're harmless as trees,

I can feel them leering. Is that not a forest?
I'm asked. Then why are there so many

tongues? I reply. I dress dutifully,
see to the clover and rabbits but as soon as my back

is turned, the trees move closer. At first axe swing,
my wrist complains and my shoulder grieves.

If I know anything, it's about loss. My blade
will need sharpening before nightfall.

I wake to a vision of Odysseus bearing
two cups of wine. Are you not thirsty? I'm asked.

Can you not come back for real? I reply. I dress dutifully
but add petals to my underthings. These petals

are another form of request. The age without
husband may allow birdsong to alight these petals

into sweet tongues. If I know desire, it's losing
its heat but will flare an impatient need

when I try fanning it out. If anything, my legs have tongue
burns that are haunting me of a matrimonial feast.

I wake hungover, my sullen tongue a warp in dried weft.
Are you alone? I was asked. Do you see anyone else?

I had replied. The lighting was poor and it had taken
a few tumblers to realize I was drinking with wolves.

I had dressed dutifully but was now alarmed
at the bounty of rabbit fur adorning me. When our server

informed us the kitchen was closed, I had gulped
secretly, fogging my composure. If I knew anything,

it was about loss not about self-defence, though when I vowed
to tear the wolves into limbs I felt a goddess stirring.

The door wakes to Telemachus. Let me in, it's told.
Its lock is diplomatic until attacked then will dutifully hold

to its bolts. Telemachus's shoulder tastes of boy
but his breath is loose with something amateurly hinged.

The door has been a surrogate father to the boy and understands
the lightening to be his personal threshold of pain. Shh, the door

nurses. It softens its wood for the boy's shoulder. This time,
he won't bruise. This time he'll recognize the door for the wood

he had whispered into. Up close, the door releases a waft of childhood
words the boy once breathed. A thankless job it does with utter devotion.

The suitors wake to me. Is this all of you? I ask. How many more can you
handle? they rooster. Your legs are one holy pair of scissors, they say.

Your hair's been licked by the sun, they say,
are you sure you're not a goddess? Mmm girl, I bet you taste

as good as you look. Though my patience is dutiful,
it sometimes pulls on its leash. There'd be no stopping that ass,

I'm told. Smile, I'm told. Show me your tits. My patience
could use a bowl of water—when the suitors finally stop,

I can hear it panting. If I know anything, I say, it's that you don't
give me joy. Come here, Penny, I'll give you joy, they chortle.

I awake, I woke   am asked

reply and say:

(dutifullydutifullydutifullydutifullydutifully)

if anything
my loss is mortal and has been acting like a goddess.

My tongue wakes to a new spice. Not as sweet as before,
is it? I'm asked. I rub the taste into the roof of my mouth,

dig into the deep wells of my teeth for the respite
of familiar taste. My tongue tests along my lips

before my mouth parts. This isn't a wound
but another slit so I may blossom. My voice surprises

me by skating. No, not skating but sliding. My name
skids past all the names, all the words said at me,

gliding with a speed that is unnerving. If everyone is stunned
it isn't because I speak, it's how my name comes out singing.

I wake to watch us. What did you do to your hair? we ask.
Our hands fledging, aloft. Nothing, we reply.

Is this the marsh of another dream or us reacquainting with the next
vow? If Odysseus is a mast, am I now a stalk, flowering?

We negotiate the distance between us with awkwardness.
When I tell him of the small hosts of lichen and my sips,

he tastes them. When he speaks the names of his lost men, I hold them
on my tongue until the names wear out their chiming. And when
    Telemachus

weeps a boy for each year his father has been gone, we open our arms
to welcome them. So many small boys clamouring for family.

from
Anthesis: A Memoir
(2020)

Burning flowers: prepare for the next season. Low chimneys
dividing dispute between farther and pure fire; exhausted
silence startled into silence. The long lament south of the sinking: a
vivid and stubborn premonition. No one remembered the exodus
from family taking every day and all night. Smoldering for her
younger edge, always more and then towards. Is the girl leaving
an emergency? She was and barely looking away.

Fuck waiting to meet the swerve, imagine nailing its danger, taking a long swig of door. The trees looked around and pressed something—a piece of paper, a poem about the waste of good meat. Imagine a cloud covering her words and missing their property line. A time portal ready to pounce. Rage grabbing the middle of the argument afterwards. The storm was genetic and thinking folded her low over anything apologizing.

She straightened her girl and ran. Her shame was right behind her
at the edge of her breath. The sound of dead leaves sneered. Where
is the last thing she didn't want to know? Panic clawed the
emergency. The green winter flinched and waited for the dark to
stop talking. Now a different landscape knew her. This recognition
sent a glimmer back to her in smoke. Once the old service moved
to the edge she couldn't see the fear. What the fuck are you

up to? She was tempted to trust her anger and threw a knife. So amazing, the hollow silence; the occasional thaw and realizing how stupid she had been. She was surprised by the land of her noise; even her breathing sounded bare. Everything herding into wild. She was looking right at the panic and the quiet knowing held her down. Out and under, under and open, over and in and scared. It didn't like protecting girls.

She could write a book about watching. Her fur, her metal detector.
The nights cleaning up after her sadness. She always asked the
same question and imagined pawing for an answer. Most days
lining up and waiting for the push and the lift. Lucky clouds that
looked like family. The green smell of crying. She wanted to
phone her name. She tried searching for the right wonder
stirring the furnace.

She looked back only once, to watch winter dig up the key. She'd only write so much worry. The lift in her mother's voice: how light it is at this hour. The word that would end the last of it. Panting and out of breath. It bellowed and slammed. Bruised the silence. Each green reaching for each other. To last longer, examining the details up close and with reverence. The blossom coaxed into and, and into summer.

from
Solstice 2020: An Archive
(2021)

December 6

The heart of December 6th isn't the soprano you'd expect but a woman able to plumb the depths of baritone for its earth and its stones. A day without hours but cellos turned with finely carved ebony pegs for how ebony is a wood that will sink in water. For this is the day tuned to the sinking. A traditional day will have many sections in its orchestra. Given the hymnal nature of December 6th, the air is softened to carry aloft fourteen young women to their future season of blossom. This isn't a ceremony but a different species of breathing. We are breathing their unfurled petals and we are breathing the further along souls that simmer above our city from so many cellos ago. The ritual of sitting down and opening our hearts for them to take haven is something we've been doing since the beginning of breath. At the heart of mourning is an inlet with small boats for us to row forward. This is the work of remembering.

December 9

The origin of laughter could probably be traced to the yodel. Hear me out. Yodel, as you know, literally means: to utter the syllable *jo* (!), blending the sacred combo of low pitch "chest noise" (the noise of the season, I think, that low baying of *wtf* and *how?*) with the higher pitch falsetto of 'head noise' (given the pandemic, this high squeal is equally all *wtf* and *how??* but wordier). There's a dumpster fire of feelings in my chest so I can only make a low noise that is on its knees tasting the distance between Halifax and Toronto; Halifax and Montreal; New York. The yodel demands this drama and the season is in the director's chair saying: *can you do it again but this time with more feeling?* What I'm really after is the amateur electrician board laugh, aka "the family gathering laugh." Sure, if the wrong wires are crossed, there could be a sudden fire but it's that danger that charges the protons and electrons of our *holy fork, I can't believe you just said that* laughs that are one of the things I'm already missing.

December 18

Consider the pinecone. Imbricated in design much like fish scales. Thin bract scales beneath seed scales. Each seed scale has two ovules; a miniature forest maker. I was tempted to use "factory" but that word has a conveyor belt for a heart and is right now churning out bladed things at an alarming rate and everyone's working overtime so all those bladed things are made in time and the coffee urn in the corner is an ancient robot spitting its orange light of being ready and there's never any real sugar but Sweet'N Low jammed into a cup and someone has to step from their spot to find the shovel because the door is jammed with snow and this dude, outside in his coveralls, bends to the task and breathes that muffler/scarf combo smell and the pinecone of feelings in his chest greens a little the way pinecones do when there's enough water and he straightens before he goes in because his back is fucked and that's when he sees this tree in the empty lot and he swears, and he takes this swearing seriously, he swears that the tree was trying to tell him something.

Afterword

An Interview with Sue Goyette and Erin Wunker

The following interview took place over several years. Begun in 2019, the interview was put on hold—like so many things—while the pandemic raged. As a document of two people talking over multiple durations—enduring, during—the following interview gives life to the compound witnessing of a poetic life.

—BV

Erin Wunker: We've decided to conduct this interview in written form so that we might give one another time to think more slowly before responding. By way of a conversation in text, then, I find I want to ask you, as a writer, teacher, and thinker, what you fortify yourself with in your writing practice. Would that be an acceptable place for us to unfurl this?

Sue Goyette: This is a good question to begin a conversation. Thank you for asking it. I've been thinking of a few things around fortifying the kind of space that helps me sustain a creative, generative approach to living in the dark times in which we find ourselves. I'd been reading about trauma-informed approaches that validate community pain, the kind we feel when we read of the species of violence and debacle that are rampant or inherently habituated and impact marginalized peoples, the planet, and, it seems, most decent and good things. I found the more I read about violence and debacle, the more my shine was dulled. It was as if I was being drawn into a doomed circuitry that was never-ending, ubiquitous, and so I stalled. Literally. I couldn't move. At first, this felt like a timely dilemma: who *could* move in this murk? And then I realized how this reflection, this rupture is filled with potential for the ways in which it disrupts a "way" and a "how" of being. If the way I'd been functioning is no longer sustainable, it means I must be in a liminal state and am, therefore, changing in a crucial way. Terrifying or exciting, depending on the lexicon.

So where does that leave me? Vulnerable. Really vulnerable and trying to move forward with curiosity rather than fear and trying to sustain tenderness because we're all facing and enduring varying degrees of loss and trauma. I'm also thinking about civic action and healing-centred engagement. To know more about that, I'm learning about caring for myself, though breaking through the guilt of taking the time to attend to my needs still sometimes feels selfish and indulged. These are clues, my friends remind me, that I'm breaking the patriarchal conditioning I've internalized. And what fortifies this way of being? Treating my body the way it needs to be treated. Walking and watering it. Moving and meditating so I feel aligned with the breath leaving and returning to me. Singing more, throwing short kitchen dance parties. Surrounding myself with good people of all ages, people who I love and who I trust. Replacing the screen for real life. Returning to therapy to be supported while I reclaim the parts of myself that I've somehow lost or forgotten and properly grieve what needs letting go as well as learning how to grieve the bigger planetary losses. Saturating myself in good music and really sharp comedy. Looking at and breathing in good art. Attending theatre that is provocative and participatory. Walking beneath trees and growing plants and flowers. Holding space for people and critters to be themselves, so attending to my biases and fears and replacing them with curiosity and gratitude. Replacing the scarcity I feel as an artist making a precarious living with generosity. Using the power I have as a cis white woman to make space for others to feel their power and agency. Finding and reading creative and/or scholarly work that is so exciting, so tenacious and chandelier-lit, I have to stand up to properly absorb it. And I try to remember daily how dazzling the world is, how genius it is in its manifesting and am amping up my trust in it and in us, because we too are capable of manifesting beyond our expectations. And mostly, I try to remember to be gentle with my fallibility. I make so many mistakes and I'm learning not to shirk the responsibility of making them.

All this helps keep the space towards poetry alert somehow to opportunities for creative risk-taking.

EW: How do you attend to the world as a writer? I am thinking, in part, of your practice of witnessing the agave in the Halifax Public Gardens in 2018. I am also thinking of a photo you posted in which moss or lichen is articulate or translated as "a method."

SG: I find myself returning to the natural world more and more for guidance and for company. Maybe it's aging. Maybe it's my understanding and appreciation for how its morphology and physiology manifest so singularly and so brilliantly. Maybe it's my version of a spiritual practice that realigns me in ways that are beyond words and grounded in body. Or all those things combined. My relationship with land is changing. I'm interested in convergent evolution and how interrelated we all are to the natural world that we participate in, and I have come to prefer multispecies conversations. This feels important to me. Historically, the intelligence of the natural world and all its inhabitants has been vastly underestimated. Complex systems like oceans and forests are harvested without care or respect or responsibility. And the consequences are dire. We're learning more about that. What would happen if that engagement changed for one that was more respectful, more interdependent? I'm putting that question into practice as often as I can and am noting some interesting changes in how I am moving in the world along with it. This practice feels important.

EW: I want to return to a place where you landed in the opening question—vulnerability. As a teacher and a writer, as a person who practices vulnerability as both life and artistic praxis, what kinds of tools of recognition do students, new poets, or long-serving poets need to listen to their own writing and living? To put this differently: how do we teach to differentiate between moments when vulnerability works as an openness and possibility for writerly practice, and when something is too raw, too soon, or when we need to hold ourselves and our aches close by a little longer?

SG: I find it helpful to acknowledge the time that has passed between the previous question you asked and this one. And how much the world has changed as we continue this conversation. We are in thrall of a global pandemic and are seeing the impact of the climate crisis, racism, poverty, a housing crisis as well as the impact of wars daily. It's been turbulent and challenging. That feeling of vulnerability we talked about is particularly active and alert right now and I first recognize it in my body for how it thrums similarly yet is distinct from fear. Perhaps I'm using vulnerability as a reframing of fear and, in a poetic context, this fear of the unknown or unknowing appears most strongly before and after I've written something new. And if this vulnerability appears at the start of something new, then perhaps it can be renamed as a sort of welcome that I'm learning more about. It's at this juncture, vulnerability as a threshold into creativity, that I'd name as a crucial tool of navigation as well as the necessary reframing of a habituated verbiage of fear in this thinking to a language that is more alert and sustainably greening.

I understand the next part of your question to be more about situating material within that praxis. My praxis has muscle memory now because I've been doing it for so long. What I've learned about the too-raw and too-soon you mention is exactly that. This writing often happens in the vortex after some hard thing. I know this by how I feel about the material, how the words I'm reaching for are doing the work of naming something that has resisted being named or is so emotionally wild, so new, it needs to be uprooted and coaxed into legibility and I'm using my writing practice as a way of rowing myself out of that difficult or challenging experience. I think the way I'm using my writing practice at this point is different or inward which, for me, isn't always something to be offered publicly. This is a private use of a practice I rely on to make clear a great many things and those things are on a spectrum that has *private* on one end and *public* on the other. Writing in this way is preliminary work and a crucial space for me to create because it offers me insight and a process of understanding. That it comes out as poetry is more about who and how I am rather than what it wants to be. Discerning what it wants to be—say, a personal textualized map or a poem—takes time and a keen reckoning. I know this work is ready to be compositionally dynamic when my perspective of the difficulty that inspired it has transformed into understanding. In this way, the material then begins to be operational for how it connects to something bigger in its thinking and is wider in its reach and offering.

EW: Your writing is alive with an unexpected linguistic choreography that nonetheless feels exacting and as though we should have always expected the adjacencies and verbal associations you make. I am thinking of Emily Dickinson's sense of the "alive" line. Can you talk a bit about how you find or conjure aliveness in your lines? How does that vitality get sustained over the course of a long poem?

SG: I really like words and sentences. And I work hard at honouring what those words are representing, what meaning they're bringing to a line, their lineage, and the light they cast, their smell, their shade, their growl, their volcanic outbursts. I like how they contribute to a syntactical cohesion. And how audacious that cohesion can be. I like how they animate that syntax and the space on the page they're taking up. How they learn to grow with each other and create their own singular logic. I also like how they work to spice the silence they're creating in all directions of themselves. This means I'm mostly watching them take root by making space for that growth rather than imposing what I think should come next or moving along in a way that I miss their potentiality entirely. So much of it is a deep and active listening and a practice of thinking along with the poem, in all directions to sustain the logic they're offering. I'm also keenly involved in how they surprise and beguile me and that feels important and delectable.

EW: I've been thinking lately of poetic hope. Not my own hope reflected in the poems I encounter, but the in-built hope of a mode of writing that refuses to follow the rules, while at the same time it projects the possibility of ordering life in different ways. Poetry, it seems to me, is equally ready to flip tables as it is prepared to invite strangers to gather around a table and share every last morsel of food available. I used to think those were opposite impulses, but now I wonder if they aren't part of the same hope. I see some of those impulses in you and your work. What are your thoughts? Do you see those complementary impulses as woven in the very fabric of poetry, of poetics?

SG: I'm really leaning into how you're thinking in this question. And am really appreciating the merits of these questions for how they say something about poetry in general and why it persists as an art form and may be the punkest of them all for how it resists commerce and enlivens us in ways it's hard to talk about. The vitality I hear in how you're using *hope* aligns with how Virginia Woolf described the alertness of words that seem to have sap. This thinking refreshes or reactivates our understanding of language and its potential, its imaginative reach and risk which, in turn, energizes us.

Wallace Stevens situates this imagination on a spectrum or in relation to reality. And here's where I feel language greening for the potential that imaginative engagement offers, how its antennae are perked and alert, on the look-out for the next potential thing. And if a poem is thinking in this way, it is invitational and, for its duration, the reader is thinking along with it and in that way can feel the sap running and embody that feeling. We are connected to it. This is no small thing, this exchange, I think, for how it can be transformative. And a recharge. So there's that.

And then there's the silence the poem is working towards and with. The silence in and around and beyond a poem is, I think, a field of the unsayable, the inexpressible. And if a poem risks getting as close as it can to that unsayable thing, then there's a deep chiming in the reader that tunes the experience of reading the poem with something they know beneath words about life, about themselves and their human and mortal heart and that acknowledgement, that recognition, recharges our dignity as humans.

I think it's at this intersection, between words and silence, where that hope you've named may be at the ready. And this experience, this connection, isn't even in the same language as the rules. Rules, in this context, are called out for what they are, a kind of fencing or ordering rather than an interrelational system that is agile and active and connective.

I also think that this creative practice makes operational a kind of radical optimism. That we can make something out of nothing is no small thing and is worthwhile to remember in the profound moments when we believe and feel like we've lost (and are losing) everything.

EW: I've got one more question for *this* iteration of (what I hope will be) our longer conversations. Indeed, I want to ask you about the way the imaginative engagement you point to has played out over time for you and your work. I guess I want to know about different ways or seasons in which that "sap" has run for you. Beginning with your first collection (*The True Names of Birds*), your poetry spans multiple modes of attention— both the poetry of the event or moment, such as "Heavy Metal Night at Gus's Pub" and the poems in *Solstice*, and poetry of the *longue durée*, such as the expanse of *Ocean*, which feels purposefully outside of human time to me. There are many more examples of a practised bifocal attention. I find I am compelled by the consistency with which you are able to switch your codes of vision while all the time committing to the role of both witness and diviner. What, for you, marks or enlivens a close or distant field of vision as imaginative engagements?

SG: In terms of commonality between my collections, Fred Moten's "writing at the outskirts of sense" comes to mind in response to "what marks or enlivens" my engagement and the commitment to that way of being that you mention. Regardless of what I'm working on, I position this way of thinking/being as a site or method I start from that reaches beyond my knowing and understanding into potential new understanding. To do this and not get lost in the ether of *all the unknowable* outside of sense that can quickly become incomprehensible and carried away on its own zeal and discovery, I find grounding myself in the real world and in this time we're in really helpful. Here's where [Wallace] Stevens's thinking about reality, imagination, and folly illuminates the way forward for me. Balancing reality and imaginative-based inquiry is a delectable creative challenge. I also am learning how to listen and observe syntactical ecosystems and patterns to better write along with them, to sustain their way of thinking and being until they come to their own natural pause or end. At the risk of sounding a little too enthusiastic, this is such a profoundly rewarding part of my writing practice, to be in the company of something becoming and moving along with it as it manifests in ways that continually surprise me.

I'm also thinking about the "field of vision" in your question for what an observational practice initiates; how it is the threshold of not only seeing more by looking but also how quickly that looking becomes relational and connective. This transformation is beneath the writing but asserts itself by how I move along with it and why. I attend to this transformative aspect of my practice for the ways it reiterates a way of being I think is important in the context of the crises mentioned above and how relationality moving towards connection and care feels especially timely and crucial. Here's that hope you mentioned. And here's when I chime in with Lucille Clifton's understanding of the universe not asking us to *be* something but asking us to *do* something. This practice delineates an operational way of connecting to the world around me with the poetic force of imaginative curiosity that leaves a trail of words for anyone who wants to inhabit those words and ways of being themselves. I guess this way of working is what I bring to the table to share with everyone.

Acknowledgements

Bart would like to thank Sue for trusting him to choose these few glimpses into a poetic life and for supporting their inclusion in this collection. It has been the best kind of work and time spent. Many thanks go to Lou Sheppard for seeing connections and for making wonderful art. Thanks also (and always) to Erin Wunker for agreeing to include her interview with Sue here and for the constant encouragement, camaraderie, and care.

Sue would like to thank Bart for his close reading and the attention he gave to her work. He has been the best reader and has given good thought to the connection and span of these poems. Thanks to Erin Wunker for asking these thought-provoking questions and to Lou Sheppard for the accompanying artwork. Sue would also like to thank Brick Books and Gaspereau Press for publishing the books these poems can be found in.

lps Books in the Laurier Poetry Series
Published by Wilfrid Laurier University Press

Don McKay *Field Marks: The Poetry of Don McKay*, edited by Méira Cook, with an afterword by Don McKay • 2006 • xxvi + 60 pp. • ISBN 978-0-88920-494-2

Duncan Mercredi *mahikan ka onot: The Poetry of Duncan Mercredi*, edited by Warren Cariou, with an afterword by Duncan Mercredi • 2020 • xx + 82 pp. • ISBN 978-1-77112-474-4

Nduka Otiono *DisPlace: The Poetry of Nduka Otiono*, selected with an introduction by Peter Midgley and an interview with Nduka Otiono by Chris Dunton • 2021 • xxii + 112 pp. • ISBN 978-1-77112-538-3

Al Purdy *The More Easily Kept Illusions: The Poetry of Al Purdy*, edited by Robert Budde, with an afterword by Russell Brown • 2006 • xvi + 80 pp. • ISBN 978-0-88920-490-4

Sina Queyras *Barking & Biting: The Poetry of Sina Queyras*, selected with an introduction by Erin Wunker, with an afterword by Sina Queyras • 2016 • xviii + 70 pp. • ISBN 978-1-77112-216-0

F.R. Scott *Leaving the Shade of the Middle Ground: The Poetry of F.R. Scott*, edited by Laura Moss, with an afterword by George Elliott Clarke • 2011 • xxiv + 72 pp. • ISBN 978-1-55458-367-6

Sky Dancer Louise Bernice Halfe *Sôhkêyihta: The Poetry of Sky Dancer Louise Bernice Halfe*, edited by David Gaertner, with an afterword by Sky Dancer Louise Bernice Halfe • 2018 • xx + 96 pp. • ISBN 978-1-77112-349-5

Fred Wah *The False Laws of Narrative: The Poetry of Fred Wah*, edited by Louis Cabri, with an afterword by Fred Wah • 2009 • xxiv + 78 pp. • ISBN 978-1-55458-046-0

Tom Wayman *The Order in Which We Do Things: The Poetry of Tom Wayman*, edited by Owen Percy, with an afterword by Tom Wayman • 2014 • xx + 92 pp. • ISBN 978-1-55458-995-1

Rita Wong *Current, Climate: The Poetry of Rita Wong*, edited by Nicholas Bradley, with an afterword by Rita Wong • 2021 • xxiv + 80 pp. • ISBN 978-1-77112-443-0

Rachel Zolf *Social Poesis: The Poetry of Rachel Zolf*, selected with an introduction by Heather Milne and an afterword by Rachel Zolf • 2019 • xviii + 80 pp. • ISBN 978-1-77112-411-9

Jan Zwicky *Chamber Music: The Poetry of Jan Zwicky*, edited by Darren Bifford and Warren Heiti, with a conversation with Jan Zwicky • 2014 • xx + 82 pp. • ISBN 978-1-77112-091-3